Starting the school year off right

Santiego Rivers

Scholars learning how to start the school year off the right way is essential because it is easier to be successful if they know how to apply themselves in the beginning and not try to catch up at the end.

Anyone who cares for our scholars' well-being should understand that we must help them develop a foundation that will foster success.

We must show them how to train their minds to be stronger than their emotions to think through every situation they will face.

We must teach them how to pray and the power that prayer has to change lives.

Evil is always present, which is why we must show them how to put on their armor each morning and stay walking in faith as they journey out off to school.

This book will give all scholars the tools that they will need to succeed in heading back to school.

Starting the school year off right

Copyright © 2021 by **Santiego Rivers**

All rights reserved. This book may not be reproduced or transmitted in any form without the written permission of the author.

"no copyright infringement is intended."

ISBN 978-1-7370516-7-1

Table of Content

First day of school checklist **(Pgs. 5-7)**

What do you want from your future? **(Pgs. 8-11)**

The difference between a scholar and a student **(Pgs.12)**

If you are present, then be present **(Pgs. 13-15)**

Things scholars know about their "entitled" teachers that students need to learn **(Pgs.16-18)**

The "Pen" vs. The "Sword" **(Pgs.19-23)**

Make them respect you **(Pgs.24-26)**

My final thoughts **(Pgs. 27-28)**

The first day of school should be a brand-new start for all scholars. Gone are the struggles of last year; the current school year brings a new beginning. Finally, scholars will be one step closer to graduation. Will they be ready?

First day of school checklist:

Is your hairdo looking good? ✓

Are your nails looking good? ✓

Are your lashes on point? ✓

Are you wearing the latest clothes? ✓

Are you wearing the latest shoes? ✓

Do you have the latest cell phone? ✓

Do you have money in your pockets? ✓

Are you ready to learn? ✗

Most scholars have the first day of school checklist that they make sure is completed upon heading back to school, while others may wing it based upon their circumstances.

Life should never be left to chance because being successful does not happen by accident.

Your checklist should not consist of how you look and what you will be wearing on the first day of school.

Your list should contain all the things that will make sure that you are going to school prepared to learn.

Your checklist should answer all the following questions and more.

Did you get enough rest the night before? Did you eat breakfast? Are you mentally prepared to return to school?

Do you have a game plan to control your emotions when things don't go your way? Are you ready to claim your success?

Having the right game plan that works for you is very important.

You must be willing to invest in your future.

Many students come to school not prepared to be scholars. Instead, they prioritize everything but what is essential.

School is not the place to be where your pockets are full, but your brain is empty.

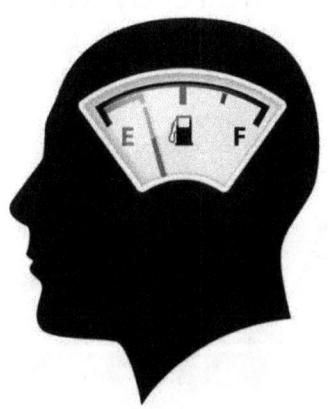

What do you want for your future?

- Do you want to graduate?
- Do you want to go to college?
- Should you go to the military?
- Should you go to a trade/ vocational school?
- Should you join the workforce after graduation?

You will not always know what you want from your life, but you should always know how you don't want your life to be.

Life has many possibilities, and some of those choices will be available to you regardless if you are ready. **(Failure)**

Regardless of how much you are loved, No one can make you want something you do not wish to have. Likewise, your parents, siblings, friends, or teachers cannot wish or pray for you to succeed in school.

When it comes to your education, it is your responsibility and no one else's.

You must have the following mindset if you plan to pursue your education or chase your dreams in life.

I am doing this for me

If you make your effort to achieve your goals based on someone else, it will leave you the option of quitting when times get tough because you did not want it for yourself.

Why I quit trying:

- *"This is what my parents wanted me to do."*
- *"I was just following my friends."*
- *"This will not help me in my future."*

Many people are afraid to give anything their whole effort because they are fearful that what they have is not enough to be successful.

To those people with this type of mindset, let me take some pressure off your shoulders by telling you the following:

Make what you have enough to be successful!

Your effort, faith, and hard work will remove all the obstacles that will stand in your way. First, however, it would help if you overcame your doubts and fears to start your path.

When you look in the mirror, you must give yourself a pep talk that will light the fire within you.

I am doing this for me

That statement means that you are willing to do whatever it takes to succeed because this is what you desire.

The difference between a student and a scholar

A **student** is primarily a person enrolled in a school or educational institution. **Scholars** are those who commit to learning willing to go above and beyond.

By emphasizing the educational aspect of their work and learning, **scholars** are appropriate; it's a way for the school district to emphasize the value and importance of the work they put into their education.

Scholars have strong motivation to use their talents and skills to benefit others rather than individual glory. But, unfortunately, **students** have yet to be inspired to commit fully to their education or their future.

Only you can determine which one you will become because you must be willing to commit yourself to learn to be a scholar.

If you are present, then be present

Many students show up to school every day but still manage to fail many of their classes. How is this possible?

It is like someone telling you that they go to work every day, but they do not have a check to show for their work when it is payday.

For a student to be failing a class that they have a high attendance in usually reflects them not applying any effort.

I am constantly telling my students that they do the most challenging part of being a scholar by showing up to school. So why not apply yourself since you are present?

Don't come to school to sit in the back of the classroom and sleep. Instead, put away your cell phone and pay more attention to what the teacher teaches you that you will need to pass the class.

Do you want to be the oldest person in the classroom because you are not applying the effort it takes to pass the class?

Is being the class clown more important than not repeating the same grade because of your lack of focus? I have some information for you that you may find interesting.

- Scholars who sit in the front of the classroom are less likely to fail their classes.
- Scholars who do not interrupt the teacher from teaching the class are less likely to fail their classes
- Scholars who are respectful towards their teachers are less likely to fail their classes.

I have just given you three ways to pass your class that had nothing to do with learning anything.

This theory comes from our current education system's flaws that allow many of our students to slip through the cracks, mostly our at-risk students.

Having passing students is more important than students learning because we pass them on to the next grade level despite them not being ready to move on.

As an educator and a behavior specialist for close to ten years, I know high school students who cannot read past an elementary school level.

I know many students perform well below their grade level but keep moving into the next grade because of the money that schools receive by having students move on to the next phase of our failing system.

Scholars, only you have the power to change this broken system.

Things scholars know about their "entitled" teachers that students need to learn

The same way that everyone you meet in the outside world will not like you is the same thing you can experience inside the classroom.

Many **"entitled"** teachers do not want you inside their classrooms. These **"entitled"** teachers will do many things to get you removed from their classroom.

The scholars that these teachers don't want in their classroom have higher referrals than average students.

I am not saying that all the referrals that these teachers write are not valid. What I am saying is that, as a Behavior Specialist and Educator, I know that many steps come before writing a referral that these teachers disregard. **(Making parent contact)**

When it comes to discipline issues with the student, teachers should contact parents or guardians by telephone.

All telephone calls to parents or guardians should be put in the school system by the teacher.

Students should be aware that those **"entitled"** teachers will teach you the difference between playing checkers and chess.

To be a good chess player, you must develop the ability to think moves ahead instead of just reacting to your opponent.

Students, you should know that once those **"entitled"** teachers learn how to push your buttons, they will do things to make you act out of character. **(Chess)**

You will react to the mental trap that they set for you because they know that your ability to think is impaired when you get upset. **(Checkers)**

Those *"entitled"* teachers will do this to justify giving you a referral that could lead to you being suspended and eventually reassigned to a secondary school. **(Chess)**

Unfortunately, many students feel that they must have the last word in every conversation/argument. These students have not learned that the *pen* will always be mightier than the *sword*. **(Checkers)**

Learning about the "pen" vs. the "sword?"

The pen is the instrument that teachers use to write the referrals that document the scholar's inappropriate actions/ behavior when they become upset.

The sword is the tongue of the upset scholar that says everything that the scholar feels when they lose control.

The student may feel that when they curse out the teacher or do some inappropriate action, it gives them some satisfaction/victory from how the teacher made them feel, making them respond negatively. **(Checkers)**

Scholars know that the harshest lesson that you should learn is that the only person who can claim satisfaction/ victory when you lose control is the person who controls the **pen. (Chess)**

The person who controls the **pen** can document how you responded when you allowed them to make you act out of character. So now the question becomes, who are you giving your power to?

When we become upset, we may act in ways that we feel is justified based on our current feeling.

What happens when we are no longer upset, and we are thinking clearer? We are then left to deal with the actions that we allowed our anger to justify.

The person who controls the **pen** will always win over the person who holds the **sword**. They learned how to think past their emotions.

Can the scholar ever get hold of the **pen**? Most schools have safeguards that allow the scholar to speak with someone when they feel upset or frustrated.

Scholars can request to speak with a school staff member to talk about issues that are bothering them.

Scholars should talk with someone at the school that can guide them could teach them how to handle a frustrating situation better and not let their anger make them act of their nature.

If the scholar cannot find help at their school, they should always turn to their parents or guardians.

Your parents or guardians can often get you the help that you need in a way that keeps you out of trouble.

Most scholars who have higher than usual referrals at school do not keep their parents informed of the challenges that they are facing.

When the scholar tries to handle a situation independently, it benefits those **"entitled"** teachers.

Most criminals are smart enough not to go into court without their attorney present, so why do you think it is okay not to use the people around you to help you be successful?

Once you realize that you are dealing with someone who does not like you, what should you do?

Make them respect you

You don't have to like your teacher, or they do not have to like you, but you both are required to show each other **respect** inside the classroom.

What is **respect**, and how should it be used between a teacher and a scholar?

Respect reflects your character and how your parents brought you up.

Respect is about treating other people the way that you want and expect them to treat you.

Respect is about having an understanding with someone that requires an agreement.

Respect is more important than love because it demands to be observed regardless of whatever emotion you are currently feeling.

You will never earn **respect** by using your sword/tongue in the classroom speaking out of anger.

A scholar will earn a teacher's **respect** or make them know that they expect to be treated fairly by communicating how they want to be treated inside the classroom.

The scholar will ensure that the teacher understands that they know their place inside the classroom and what the classroom expectations are.

The scholars will agree to follow the classroom rules and not stop the educator from teaching their class.

The scholar will reiterate that they want to feel comfortable inside the classroom and be taught in the learning style that helps them learn the needed material. Always begin your conversation with, "With all due respect," and end-all of your conversations with a smile.

Success doesn't happen by accident. It takes faith, hard work, planning, and sacrifice to make it happen.

You can't pray for victory while continuing to operate in defeat.

It would help if you learned how to be ready for when that moment presents itself to take full advantage of it.

My final thoughts

Many students may feel that no one cares about them being successful in life. But, hopefully, after reading this book or any other book that I have written to inspire you to achieve success at your level, you know that one person does care about you.

You know another person who cares about you also. Whoever saw fit to give you any of my material to read wanted to get your attention.

The easiest thing for most people to do in the presence of wrongdoing is to remain silent.

The hardest thing for someone to do when they witness an injustice happening in their presence is to remain quiet.

Doing the right thing is not always the most popular thing to do, but it is the most rewarding thing that anyone can do for humanity.

I use my writing to shout from the mountain top, hoping that it will travel to the destination it will do the most good.

You are the intended audience. So, naturally, we want you to have the chance to be successful, but it is up to you to apply the needed effort.

This book removes your ability to say that you were not taught how to be successful when you return to school.

After reading this book, you can only say that you did not apply the lessons/ skills that the book taught you about success when you return to school.

No more excuses!!!

www.ingramcontent.com/pod-product-compliance
Lightning Source LLC
Chambersburg PA
CBHW071014160426
43193CB00012B/2050